NATURE'S CHILDREN

ELEPHANTS

by Francis Brennan

Children's Press®

An Imprint of Scholastic Inc.
New York   Toronto   London   Auckland   Sydney
Mexico City   New Delhi   Hong Kong
Danbury, Connecticut

Content Consultant
Dr. Stephen S. Ditchkoff
Professor of Wildlife Sciences
Auburn University
Auburn, Alabama

Photographs © 2013: Alamy Images: 1, 2 foreground, 16, 46
(AfriPics.com), 4, 5 background, 27 (Ann and Steve Toon), 40
(Claudia Wiens); Bob Italiano: 44 foreground, 45 foreground;
Dreamstime/Steffen Foerster: 2 background, 3, 44 background,
45 background; Getty Images/Chris Caldicott: 5 top, 8; Photo
Researchers/Anthony Bannister: 36; Shutterstock, Inc.: cover (clickit),
11 (Graeme Shannon), 20 (indiangypsy), 23 (Irina Ivanova), 19
(Johan Swanepoel), 12 (Peter Betts), 15 (Steve Allen), 5 bottom, 28
(Steve Bower), 7 (TebNad); Superstock, Inc.: 24 (age fotostock),
31 (De Agostini), 39 (Frans Lemmens), 32 (Hanan Isachar), 35
(imagebroker.net).

Library of Congress Cataloging-in-Publication Data
Brennan, Francis, 1980–
  Elephants/by Francis Brennan.
    p. cm.—(Nature's children)
  Includes bibliographical references and index.
  ISBN-13: 978-0-531-26833-9 (lib. bdg.)
  ISBN-13: 978-0-531-25478-3 (pbk.)
  1. Elephants—Juvenile literature. I. Title.
  QL737.P98B746 2013
  599.67—dc23   2012000639

All rights reserved. Published in 2013 by Children's Press, an imprint
of Scholastic Inc.
Printed in China 62
SCHOLASTIC, CHILDREN'S PRESS, and associated logos are
trademarks and/or registered trademarks of Scholastic Inc.

1 2 3 4 5 6 7 8 9 10 R 22 21 20 19 18 17 16 15 14 13

Elephants

Class	Mammalia
Order	Proboscidea
Family	Elephantidae
Genus	*Elephas* (Asian elephants) and *Loxodonta* (African elephants)
Species	*Elephas maximus* (Asian elephants), *Loxodonta africana* (savanna elephants), and *Loxodonta cyclotis* (forest elephants)
World distribution	Asian elephants are found in eastern, southern, and southeastern Asia; savanna elephants are found in eastern and southern Africa; forest elephants are found in western and central Africa
Habitats	Grasslands, savannas, tropical forests, and woodlands
Distinctive physical characteristics	Very large animals with large ears, a trunk, and thick skin
Habits	Daily bathing; coverage of skin in dirt; females live in familial groups; adult males live most of their lives in solitude
Diet	A variety of plant parts, including bark, branches, fruit, grasses, herbs, leaves, and roots

Contents

CHAPTER 1

Thundering Across the Plains

A light breeze blows through the grasses of an African savanna. Suddenly, the silence is broken by loud, distant trumpeting. The ground shakes and trees sway. The noises grow louder as a herd of elephants thunder toward a nearby watering hole for a drink and a bath.

Elephants are best known for their enormous size. In fact, the African elephant is the largest land animal on Earth. African elephants reach heights of about 8 to 10.5 feet (2.4 to 3.2 meters) on average. They are also incredibly heavy. The largest elephant on record weighed about 24,000 pounds (10,886 kilograms). This is more than a hundred times the weight of an average adult man.

Adult Male
6 ft. (1.8 m)

Adult Elephant
10.5 ft. (3.2 m)

Elephant herds are a common sight in many parts of the African savanna.

Not Quite the Same

There are three different species of elephants. The African savanna elephant and the African forest elephant are found in different parts of Africa. These two species are very closely related. Until the early 2000s, most scientists organized them together as a single species. Forest elephants are slightly smaller than their savanna relatives and have slimmer tusks. They also live in different environments. Forest elephants are found mainly in wooded rain forest areas, while savanna elephants roam Africa's grasslands.

The third elephant species is the Asian elephant. It can be found throughout Asian countries such as India and Indonesia. Asian elephants are smaller than either of the two other species. They only grow to about 6.6 to 9.8 feet (2 to 3 m) tall and weigh less than 11,023 pounds (5,000 kg). But size is not the only way to tell Asian and African elephants apart. Asian elephants have smaller, less floppy ears than the two African species. Female Asian elephants do not usually have visible tusks, but it is easy to spot these long teeth on both genders in African elephants.

Female Asian elephants have very small tusks, which do not stick out of their mouths.

CHAPTER 2

Striving to Survive

In the wild, healthy adult elephants have no known predators. Other animals usually do their best to stay out of an elephant's way. In combat, a fully grown elephant can usually crush any other animal. However, young, injured, or sick elephants are vulnerable to attacks from lions. When an elephant finds itself in a dangerous situation, it makes loud noises and lifts its trunk to show off its mighty tusks. These huge, curved teeth are used to fight off many potential threats.

Tusks are not only for fighting off enemies. Elephants sometimes use them to dig in the ground for water. They also use them to remove bark from trees so they can eat it. Tusks are handy for plowing through branches and trees when clearing a path through a thick forest. Occasionally, elephants also use their tusks to play or fight with each other.

Male elephants wrestle using their tusks and trunks.

Elephant Senses

Elephants have very poor eyesight. However, this doesn't mean they can't tell what is going on around them. Some scientists have even observed herds being led by elephants that were completely blind!

Instead of using their eyes, elephants mostly rely on sound, smell, and touch to navigate and search for food. Their huge ears give them an excellent sense of hearing. Elephants can hear many sounds that are far too low for human ears to detect.

Elephants are often seen raising their long trunks up above their heads and waving them back and forth through the air. Scientists believe that elephants do this to gather useful information from scents.

Elephants are also highly sensitive to vibrations in the air or along the ground. They can feel these rumblings with their trunks and feet. This helps them locate other elephants from very far away.

An elephant's trunk is one of its most important sensory organs.

Thick Skin

Elephants are known for their tough, wrinkly skin. Around most parts of the body, this skin is 1 inch (2.5 centimeters) thick. Even though it is very strong, elephant skin is also quite sensitive. An elephant can feel the touch of a single fly landing on its body.

Because their skin is so sensitive, elephants must take care to protect it from sunburn and bug bites. They must also make sure it doesn't get too dry. One way they do this is by wallowing in mud. The mud is soothing and healthy for their skin. Elephants also protect their skin with a behavior known as dusting. First, the elephant takes a bath in a pool of water or uses its trunk to spray water onto its body. Then the elephant uses its trunk to throw dirt all over its wet body. The dirt sticks to the water and forms a protective covering as it dries.

FUN FACT! An elephant's trunk can hold up to 1.6 gallons (6 liters) of water at a time.

Mud keeps elephants cool and protects their skin.

Play It Cool

Elephants must work to stay cool. Taking baths or wallowing in mud can help them beat the heat, but such activities are not enough on their own. An elephant's ears are its main tools for lowering its body temperature. These huge, floppy ears are made up mainly of thin layers of skin stretched across cartilage and a huge web of tiny blood vessels.

When they are feeling warm, elephants get their ears wet and then flap them to create a breeze. This breeze cools the blood flowing through their ears. As the cooled blood makes its way through the elephant's body, the elephant's body temperature begins to drop.

Elephants that live in warmer environments have larger ears. This is why African elephants have much bigger ears than their Asian relatives.

An elephant's ears are like built-in air conditioners.

On the Move

Even though elephants are huge, they do not move as slowly as you might think. Elephants usually walk at a rate of about 4.5 miles per hour (7.2 kilometers per hour). They can keep up that pace for hours on end. Elephant herds have been known to cover 50 miles (80.5 km) in a day's march.

Elephants have large, round feet to support the incredible weight of their bodies. Each foot has a thick layer of fat at the heel, to provide cushioning as the elephant walks.

When an elephant feels threatened, it can move as swiftly as 25 miles per hour (40 kph). When a whole group of elephants becomes frightened and begins to run, it is called a stampede. Elephants can only run at top speeds for a few minutes at a time, so stampedes do not last long. However, they can cause tremendous damage in that short time. Elephant stampedes can be very dangerous for people living in towns or villages near elephant habitats.

Elephant herds can kick up a lot of dust during a stampede.

CHAPTER 3

Life in the Herd

An elephant herd is usually made up of several **generations** of closely related female elephants, along with their very young male relatives. Each herd is led by a **matriarch**. She is usually the oldest elephant in the herd.

Elephants often travel long distances to find food. The matriarch uses her years of experience to lead her herd on these journeys. She is able to remember an area's **geography** and can direct her relatives to places where food is plentiful.

When a herd grows too large, some of the older members break away to form their own group. These related herds remain friendly with each other but travel separately. They become very excited when they meet in the wilderness.

Except for when they are very young, male elephants do not generally live in herds. They usually live alone and meet up with females when it comes time to **mate**. However, males sometimes travel together in groups called bachelor herds.

The matriarch uses her wisdom to make sure her herd stays healthy and free from danger.

Having a Chat

Elephants are very social animals. They enjoy each other's company and often form very deep bonds with their family members. They have many ways of communicating with one another. They can make a wide variety of sounds, ranging from low growls and roars to high-pitched cries. They are most famous for the loud, trumpetlike noises they make with their trunks. They use these sounds to express their feelings, warn family members of danger, and point out food sources.

Elephants also produce very low rumbling noises in their stomachs. These sounds are too low for human ears to hear. They let other elephants know that there are no threats nearby.

Elephants also communicate by touching each other. Family members are very affectionate toward one another. They often rub their bodies together or hold on to each other's trunks. Baby elephants and their mothers touch almost constantly.

Elephants use their trunks to show friendship and affection toward one another.

A Meal and a Nap

Elephants are **herbivores**. They eat bark, branches, fruit, grasses, herbs, leaves, and roots. Older elephants usually eat softer plant parts. This is because elephants' teeth wear down as they age, making it harder to chew tough plants.

Because they are so large and grow so quickly, elephants must eat huge amounts of food. An elephant eats about 220 to 440 pounds (100 to 200 kg) of food every day. It washes these huge meals down with about 30 gallons (114 liters) of water per day. It can take a long time to find and eat this much food. Elephants spend about three-quarters of their lives eating!

Because of the amount of time they spend feeding, elephants sleep for only about four hours a day. About half of that time is spent sleeping while standing up. Elephants only lie down during the deepest sleep. During this part of their slumber, they often snore loudly.

Elephants stand on their back legs to reach low-hanging fruits and leaves.

Mating Season

Elephant mating season lasts for about three weeks each year. However, females are only fertile for three to five days during this time. When a female elephant is ready to mate, she temporarily leaves her herd and begins to produce scents and make noises that attract males.

Female elephants prefer to mate with large, strong males. This means they usually mate with elephants that are older than they are. When a male is attracted by a female's scents and sounds, he approaches and begins the courtship process. If the female is not interested, she will run away. If she is interested, she will soon join in the courtship by nuzzling or touching the male with her trunk.

Sometimes more than one male becomes interested in the same female. These males compete with each other to prove which one is the strongest. They ram into one another and use their tusks to fight, but are rarely injured during these competitions.

Male and female elephants show their affection toward each other during the courtship process.

Bringing Up Baby

A baby elephant is born about 22 months after its parents mate. Newborn elephants receive a lot of attention from their mothers and other herd members. They gather around the baby as soon as it is born and touch it with their trunks. Even though it is just a baby, it is still quite large. Newborn elephants are about 3.3 feet (1 m) tall and weigh around 220 pounds (100 kg).

Elephants are almost blind when they are first born. They rely on their trunks to sense what is going on around them. They are born with few survival instincts. Instead, they must learn important skills from the older elephants in their herds.

Allomothers are other herd members that help the mother care for her baby. They walk with the baby as the herd travels, helping it if it falls or gets stuck in the mud. They also protect it from enemies.

Baby elephants are very playful.

CHAPTER 4

Elephants of the Past

While there are only three species in the elephant family living today, others existed long ago. One example is the mammoth. Mammoths were about the same size as today's elephants, but they were covered in thick fur and had much smaller ears. Because they usually lived in cold areas, they did not need big ears to help cool down their bodies. They once lived on every continent except for South America and Australia, but they slowly disappeared from some areas. By about 11,000 years ago, they could only be found in North America. Soon after, they died out completely.

Even though they went **extinct** thousands of years ago, scientists know a lot about these ancient elephants. This is because they left behind many **fossils**. Some mammoths were also preserved in blocks of ice. They sometimes died after getting trapped in huge cracks in the ice. They were then covered over with more ice.

Fossils and other remains have helped scientists learn a lot about mammoths.

A History with Humans

Humans have a long and complicated relationship with elephants. These huge, intelligent animals have captured the attention of people for thousands of years. They were a common subject of ancient cave paintings in Europe. Many civilizations throughout history used them to help with military and construction tasks. Some continue to do so even today. In Burma and Thailand, armies use elephants to remove trees and transport logs. In India, elephants are sometimes used as a method of transportation.

Elephants are celebrated for more than just their strength and ability to work. In Asia, elephants are used in a variety of religious ceremonies. They are often present at weddings and other important events. Some followers of the Hindu religion worship a god named Ganesh. Ganesh has the body of a man and the head of an elephant.

Cave paintings, such as this one in Israel, show that humans have been interacting with elephants for thousands of years.

CHAPTER 5

Now and Forever?

Today, elephant populations are very low in certain parts of the world. This is mostly a result of human actions. As human populations have grown, elephants have suffered. Elephants living in the wild must struggle against the threats of illegal hunting, habitat loss, and pollution. Others are forced to live in zoos or perform in circuses. Elephants do not react well to captivity. They need space to move, and they become very unhappy if they cannot socialize with other elephants.

African forest elephants face a unique danger that other species do not have to deal with. Many of the places where they live have seen a great deal of violence over the past several decades. People living in these areas have often battled each other for control of natural resources or government leadership. Elephants and other animals end up caught in the crossfire, with nowhere to go.

Many captive elephants are forced to perform tricks in circuses.

The Problem with Poaching

Poaching is another major problem for elephants. Mankind has long hunted elephants for their **ivory**. Records of this practice date back at least 3,500 years. Ivory has been used to create billiard balls, piano keys, jewelry, and artwork. Owning ivory was once an important status symbol for wealthy people. Hunters wiped out huge numbers of elephants to meet the demand for their tusks. Between 1970 and 1989, hunters decreased the population of African elephants from about 1,300,000 to about 600,000. Some countries have banned the trade of ivory, but others continue to allow it today.

Elephants have been known to strike back against the humans who attack them. They sometimes raid villages in Africa and India, attacking people, destroying buildings, and eating entire fields of crops. About 500 people die in these raids each year. Some scientists believe that the elephants kill people on purpose. They think that elephants might be able to recognize groups of people who attacked their relatives.

Many poachers are willing to kill elephants just to harvest their tusks.

Nowhere to Go

Habitat loss is an even bigger problem than poaching. As towns, cities, and villages continue to grow in Africa and Asia, people take over land that was once home to elephants and other animal species. The elephants do not have enough space to live, and there is less food for them to eat. In some areas, authorities are even considering killing large numbers of elephants to reduce the population size and make more room for humans.

Mining, oil, and timber companies have pushed work camps far into the forests of Africa and Asia. They build roads to connect the camps to towns and cities. These roads cause two major problems for elephants. First, they allow poachers to easily travel into the forest. Second, they block elephants from traveling freely. Some elephants end up stuck in small areas of land that are surrounded by roads and other structures. They do not have room to search for food or find mates.

Elephants are sometimes forced to work on the same logging projects that are destroying their habitats.

Safety in Sanctuaries

Scientists, government officials, and everyday people are all working together to help protect elephants from these dangers. Elephant sanctuaries provide space for elephants to live in the wild without fear of poachers or habitat loss. Workers at sanctuaries provide food and water, and make sure the elephants stay happy and healthy. Some sanctuaries allow visitors, while others are closed to the public.

Many sanctuaries, such as those in India and Thailand, are located in places where elephants live naturally in the wild. Others can be found in faraway locations such as Tennessee and Arkansas. Despite their distance from native habitats, the weather at the U.S. sanctuaries is not all that different from the weather in the elephants' natural homes.

In addition to providing homes for elephants, sanctuaries work to spread awareness of the problems facing these beautiful, intelligent animals. With any luck, such efforts will help to create a world where people treat elephants with the care and respect they deserve.

Sanctuaries make sure that elephants will have places to live and grow for many years to come.

Words to Know

allomothers (AH-loh-muhth-urz) — herd members who help a mother elephant care for her baby

captivity (kap-TIV-i-tee) — the condition of being held or trapped by people

cartilage (KAR-tih-lidj) — tough elastic tissue

courtship (KORT-ship) — the process in which an animal expresses its interest in mating

environments (en-VYE-ruhn-mints) — surroundings in which an animal lives or spends time

extinct (ik-STINGKT) — no longer found alive

fertile (FUR-tuhl) — able to have babies

fossils (FOSS-uhlz) — the hardened remains of prehistoric plants and animals

generations (jen-uh-RAY-shuhnz) — animals or individuals born around the same time

geography (jee-AH-gruh-fee) — the physical features of an area

habitats (HAB-uh-tats) — the places where an animal or a plant is usually found

herbivores (HUR-buh-vorz) — animals that only eat plants

herd (HURD) — a group of animals that stays together or moves together

instincts (IN-stingkts) — natural behaviors or responses

ivory (EYE-vur-ee) — a hard, whitish substance that forms the tusks of mammals, especially elephants

mate (MAYT) — to join together to produce babies

matriarch (MAY-tree-ark) — an experienced female elephant who leads her herd

poaching (POH-ching) — hunting or fishing illegally

pollution (puh-LOO-shuhn) — harmful materials that damage or contaminate the air, water, and soil

sanctuaries (SANGK-choo-er-eez) — natural areas where animals are protected from hunters or other dangers

savanna (suh-VAN-uh) — a flat, grassy plain with few or no trees

species (SPEE-sheez) — one of the groups into which animals and plants of the same genus are divided

stampede (stam-PEED) — a sudden, wild rush of animals in one direction, usually caused by fear

trunk (TRUHNGK) — the long nose of an elephant

tusks (TUHSKS) — the long, curved, pointed teeth that stick out of the mouths of animals such as elephants, walruses, or wild boars

wallowing (WAH-loh-ing) — rolling around in mud or water

NORTH

AMERICA

PACIFIC

ATLANTIC

OCEAN

SOUTH
AMERICA

Elephant Range

ARCTIC OCEAN

EUROPE

ASIA

AFRICA

PACIFIC OCEAN

OCEAN

INDIAN OCEAN

AUSTRALIA

Find Out More

Books

Downer, Ann. *Elephant Talk: The Surprising Science of Elephant Communication*. Minneapolis: Twenty-First Century Books, 2011.

Firestone, Mary. *Top 50 Reasons to Care About Elephants*. Berkeley Heights, NJ: Enslow Publishers, 2010.

Marsh, Laura. *Elephants*. Washington, DC: National Geographic, 2010.

O'Connell, Caitlin, and Donna M. Jackson. *The Elephant Scientist*. Boston: Houghton Mifflin, 2011.

Sexton, Colleen. *The African Elephant*. Minneapolis: Bellwether Media, 2012.

Visit this Scholastic Web site for more information on elephants:
www.factsfornow.scholastic.com
Enter the keyword **Elephants**

Index

About the Author

Francis "Chech" Brennan studied music and literature at Purchase College. He currently resides in New York City, where he works as a musician and writer. This is his first book.